MW01615919

Arise and Thrive: A Holistic Health Devotional

Copyright © 2023 by Amy Miller

ISBN 978-1-7388473-1-0 (Softcover)
ISBN 978-1-7388473-0-3 (eBook)

All Scripture Quotations, unless otherwise indicated, are from the ESV® Bible (The Holy Bible, English Standard Version®). Copyright © 2001 by Crossway, a publishing ministry of Good News Publishers. Used by Permission. All rights reserved.

Scripture taken from the HOLY BIBLE, NEW INTERNATIONAL VERSION®. Copyright ©1973, 1978, 1984, by International Bible Society. Used by permission of Zondervan. All rights reserved.

Citation from 'Breaking Free From Body Shame,' by Jess Connolly. Used by Permission.

All Photographs used via Canva.com © kswelty from Getty Images; © Susanne906 from Pixabay; ©Kat72 from Getty Images; © Thomas_Zsebok_Images from Getty Images Pro; © Sharocks from Getty Images; © Amine Toumi from Getty Images; © Matt_Gibson from Getty Images; © Jonathan Petersson from Pexels; © MLZD from l'equipe de choc; © Qimono from Pixabay; © Elandis-Patrick; © Rohit Gangwar; © Irina Iriser from Pexels; © Scott Webb from Pexels; © OGPhoto from Getty Images; © Ostseekinder from Pixabay; © PeopleImages from Getty Images; © Kenneth Carpina from Pexels; © Peter Veenendaal from Getty Images; © Racide from Getty Images; © Pexels--2286921 from Pixabay; © Gyro from Getty Images; © Hirurg from Getty Images; © Olandsfokus; ©12019 from Pixabay; © Beeldbewerking from Getty Images; © Kurmyshov from Getty Images; © Pok_Rie from Pixabay; © Geralt from Pixabay; © Lum3n from Pexels; © Larisa-K from Pixabay; © Scopio Images.

Printed in Canada

Published By Amy Miller
75 Doherty Close
Red Deer, AB T4R 3G1

www.ariseandthrivecoaching.ca

This life was not meant to just be 'survived,' yet that's how many people function. Why is that? Why are we running from place to place 'surviving?' It's evident from Scripture that God has created us not to survive, but rather to Thrive.

At times we find ourselves in a barren season that seems like no growth or thriving is possible. Is there a way to Thrive in these seasons? I believe - Yes!

The basis of this devotional is that we have been created to Thrive. We are the crowning masterpiece of God's creation. He has called us to "live life to the full," as is stated in John 10:10. Jeremiah 29:11 declares that the plans He has for us are good and for our future. He wants and can do immeasurably more than we can ask or imagine as seen in Ephesians 3:20. This is God's desire for us and the invitation of this devotional - to Thrive as God has created you to. However, even though God has given us all things for life and godliness, our responsibility is to step up into the life He has called us to. Our part is to Arise.

The terminology of 'Arise' comes from Isaiah 61, when the Lord tells His people to "Arise and shine, for your light has come and the glory of the Lord has risen upon you." It sounds wonderful, but the reality was that Isaiah had been talking about the destruction and exile of Israel for most of the book before the final chapters of hope. The way that Isaiah 61 is worded is in the complete form - that these things have happened and are the reality. But they didn't see it yet. The same is true in our lives. The reality is that Jesus has won and is victorious. He has not only created us to Thrive, but has also made a way for us to Thrive through His blood, but are we stepping into it?

The call to Arise throughout this devotional is really about partnering with God to do hard things. It's about knowing who God is, who we are and what we're created for (ie. Thriving). This foundational knowledge is to spur us on to step into Thriving by aligning with God's truth to change our minds, as well as discipline through action. The image that I see for us is that we would lift our heads high out of the pit, see the way out that Jesus has made and start taking those steps with His help. The image of Arising lends itself to the fact that there's something to rise up under or to climb out of - that's what this devotional is intended to help with. That you would indeed Arise under your burden to do the hard things with the help of our Creator so that we may truly step into His desire for us to Thrive.

Throughout the first five weeks of devotionals, we focus on developing spiritual health disciplines by getting into the Bible at least five times per week. Further, the devotionals are focused on aligning our minds and thoughts with truth in regards to holistic health. To help solidify the reading for each day, there are daily action items suggested because our society is rich in information, but the action aspect can be scarce. These 'Stick it with Action' items are meant to be a simple kickstart to Arise in the face of challenge to bring about Thriving.

Further, we will prepare our minds for change by diving into Truth throughout the first five weeks so that we are ready to move on to planning for change through goal setting. The goal setting stage will be full of reflection and evaluation to reveal where you're at and to help you establish a plan that works for you to create healthy habits that bring about holistic health and the opportunity to Thrive. The last few weeks of the devotional are meant to take you on a journey of discovering what God has put in you, where you're at, what you need to overcome and ultimately how you may need to Arise in order to Thrive.

My deep desire is to see women living life to the full as God has created us. But in order to do that, sometimes we need to do hard things and to rise up under the load we find ourselves buried by. As we embrace the hard, we will develop new strength to Arise and Thrive. May you enjoy the journey.

Table of Contents
CONTENTS

Created to Thrive

WEEK 1

DAY 1

God is Good

Verse Challenge

Take some time and read Ephesians 1:3-14. Take note and write down what God has done for us and given us. Then write down the motivation and purpose for why God has done these things.

We're going to start with the very basics, because the reality is that we can never get away from the basics. Just like you can't build a house without a firm foundation, we can't build a solid life apart from foundational truths.

Every time I read this passage, I need to read it a few times to start to grasp the depth of what God has done for me. I know what He's done, but this causes me to slow down and ask if I REALLY know it.

This passage clearly declares that the God of the universe chose US! He chose us to be holy and blameless, to know the mystery of Christ, to be forgiven and adopted. The crazy thing is that forgiveness and adoption required everything of Him - it required sacrifice. Further, as you keep sifting through this passage, you start to take note of the all encompassing language - 'every spiritual blessing,' 'all wisdom,' 'to bring unity to all things'... The comprehensive emphasis of the passage describes and matches God's action. He sacrificed Himself and He continues to give all of Himself to us in the Holy Spirit. He not only gave Himself FOR us, but now lives IN us!

But why? Yes, to make us holy and blameless, but what was His motivation? Do you see it at the end of verses 4 and 5, and then again in verse 9? His motivation was love. The NIV describes His motivation beautifully saying it was because of 'His good pleasure!' Let this sink in - it delights Him to lavish His love upon us!

The reason we need to start here is because sometimes in the mundane, or the barren, or the hardship, we can be lulled to sleep and forget these profound truths.

But the reality is this - GOD IS GOOD!

This Good God has given you all of Himself! He wants to do life with you! He wants to infuse you with His love, joy and passion. He has created you to not just survive, but Thrive!

Challenge to Apply

Take some time to reflect on and thank God for how Good He is as we begin this journey to Arise and Thrive!

Stick it with Action

Create some space today to go outside and sit or walk for 5 min. Invite the Lord to to make you aware of His presence. Walk slowly and breathe deeply. Allow space for your senses to come to life. What do you see, what do you hear, what do you smell, what do you feel? Take a moment to stand still and be conscious of the fact that God created these sights, sounds, smells and feelings for you at this particular moment! Praise God for all that He has done, but more than that, praise Him for Who He Is.

Verse Challenge

Read Mark 5:24-34 and note Jesus' reaction, intention and words in response to the woman's boldness.

Delighted In
DAY 2

The two years of Covid lockdowns were hard ones for so many reasons, but one glaring hardship for me was the lack of personal interaction. My second son was born two weeks into the first lockdown. I'm not going to lie, it was a hard pill to swallow and sometimes still is when I think about the fact that so many people didn't meet him as a newborn and he that wasn't celebrated like a new baby should be due to the restrictions. It felt like he was overlooked.

Sometimes we can feel overlooked by God, but when I read Scripture I the truth that we are seen is evident.

At times, it can be hard to put ourselves into the shoes of the person we're reading about in Scripture. One lady in the Bible who seemed overlooked was the woman who suffered from bleeding for twelve years. I remember when this account gripped me for the first time. Think about it:

- She had her period for twelve years! I hate it on a monthly basis, let alone for twelve years! What was her flow like? How did they deal with that 'time of the month' in Biblical times?

- Her cramps must've been bad, because it says that she spent all that she had on physicians trying to get better yet they only made it worse. Talk about frustration with the 'health care system.' She had unknown ailments and only to got a situation that was worse physically than before, which left her destitute.
- But the worst thing would have been the fact that she was 'unclean.' Women on their menstrual cycle were considered 'unclean' and the ramifications of being 'unclean' in that society were that you were removed from the community and put into social isolation. Further, someone or something unclean could make other things unclean. With that in mind - I wonder how long she had gone without a hug from someone.

If anyone had a right to be bitter or give up hope - it was this woman. But then she heard about Jesus, and hope flickered once again. Actually, hope started to burn a little hotter than it had in years. That hope and belief caused her to be in a crowd that she shouldn't have been in. It caused her to not only be there, but actually have the audacity to touch the bottom hem of Jesus' clothes. And because of her bold action, faith healed her physically!

But Jesus wasn't done - He wanted to heal the deep parts of her soul. So he asked "who touched me?" The disciples looked at Him like He was mad because everyone was 'touching him' (as if they were in a crowd waiting to see Oprah!) But Jesus persisted until she came forward. It says that she was scared, and told Him everything. I can only imagine the fear in her heart as she confessed to being unclean and having touched Him - what would He do? Would He shame her? Would He rebuke her? Would He reverse the healing that had taken place? His response silenced all of those fears with His first word, 'Daughter.'

I think in that moment, Jesus healed way more than anyone would ever know. We see this over and over again in Scripture where Jesus heals someone physically, but then proceeds to heal emotionally, mentally and spiritually. Why? Because Jesus is deeply concerned about our whole being.

In that moment, this woman knew that she was seen, known, and LOVED by her Heavenly Father!

Challenge to Apply

Do you feel overlooked today? Or maybe you're dealing with emotions of rejection? Maybe you just don't know where God is in your situation. Can I encourage you to write those out today, give them to the Father, and ask Him to speak His truth over you. Ask the Holy Spirit to make the fact that you are a Beloved Daughter of the King real in your heart today. The ability to Arise starts with owning your identity - that you are delighted in - and from there we're able to Thrive.

Stick it with Action

Today, take a bit of time to put your make up on. Instead of rushing through it, take time to enjoy the process. Invite the Lord to come and speak His words of truth over you. Ask Him to reveal to you how He sees you, rather than being stuck on what you see. Once your make up is done, either make a coffee or go grab a coffee and enjoy a date with the One who delights in you.

DAY 3

Life to the full

We live in a day and age where information and entertainment is at everyone's fingertips. It's an age where we crave and need entertainment. Social media plays on this and we end up scrolling way longer than we ever intend because we're captivated by the highlight reels of everyone else's life.

Then we come back to reality, and we wonder why our life lacks luster...

I'm not saying that social media is bad. There are actually some incredible ways that we're able to use social media, but sometimes it causes dissatisfaction with the life we have and I don't believe that's what God desires.

In fact, I know that God has incredible things for us.

John 10:10 is one of my favourite verses in the Bible. It says that Jesus came to not just give us Life, but life to the FULL!

Growing up, it felt like we always focused on Jesus dying on the cross for our salvation so that we can go to Heaven. But that's not what this passage is saying. Rather, this passage is talking about a relationship with the Good Shepherd where we hear His voice and respond to what He has for us. He wants to give us Abundant Life. Not just for eternity but for TODAY!

How many of us feel like we're not living abundant life though? I know for me as a mom of toddlers, I can feel like I'm caught in groundhog day; I'm stuck in the mundane, and there's nothing glamorous about it... That is until I let God infuse these days with HIS Abundance, then the mundane becomes a sacred training ground for the future.

What I've realized is that Abundant life can sometimes come down to a matter of perspective. Scripture talks often about guarding your heart, thoughts and mind. Why? Because out of our thoughts become actions which dictate the direction of our life. In this season of mundane, I've decided to make it a training ground for patience, perseverance, as well as a season of planting for the future. With that in mind, all of a sudden 'nap-prison' has meaning, purpose and an element of excitement!

What season of life are you in? Are you living life to the full? Are you mostly positive or negative about your lot in life currently? Ask the Holy Spirit to reveal and convict you about any negative perspectives and repent of those. Replace your negative perspectives by writing the ways that you are Thriving. Then lay the areas that you desire to Arise and Thrive in before the Lord asking for His infusion of life so that you may live to the full.

Stick it with Action

Arising and Thriving has a growth aspect to it. It starts small with seemingly nothing, but slowly growth comes and over time a beautiful flower will bloom. In light of today's devotional on living life to the full, get some flowers to arrange, buy an arrangement of flowers, or flower seeds to plant. Let these remind you of who you are and what you've been created for - to Thrive.

Read Mark 1:29-39 and write down what Jesus' purpose was and how He carried out that purpose.

I don't know about you, but sometimes it's easy to look at Jesus in the Gospels and assume that life was easier for Him. Of course He could've gotten up early to spend time in prayer because He was God. Of course He could love others because He was God. Of course He knew what His purpose was, He was God...

However, when we do this, we minimize the fact that Jesus was 100% human. Jesus put aside Godlike qualities to fully be in the confines of a man.

The passage we read today gives us insight into Jesus' purpose and how He fulfilled it. He came to 'proclaim good news to the poor, freedom for the prisoners, recovery of sight for the blind, and to set the oppressed free' (Luke 4:18, Isaiah 61:1-2). We cannot overlook the humanity of Jesus in this though. He was human like us, and when you are ministering to people constantly, you get tired, even if you're an extrovert.

I love the series 'The Chosen' because the writing and acting paint a beautiful picture of Jesus' humanity. He required food; He got exhausted; He had emotions. One episode in the second season portrayed His humanity in such raw fashion. A day of intense ministry and healing was painted where He was on His feet all day, putting other people's needs above His own. He didn't come back to camp until late in the evening, limping and struggling. The image of His humanity was tangible; He wore out like us, and became exhausted at times.

How did He keep going? Did He take a day off? Did He sleep in? Did claim a day of 'self-care'? Yes, He did take naps, and He did get away from the crowds at times, but the consistent habit we see in this passage and others is that He woke up early to pray. He did not go to pray because He was God, but rather in light of the very fact that He was human, He went to commune with the Father to strengthen Him for the day ahead.

Jesus came not only to save us, but He came as a man to show us what it looks like to Arise and Thrive. He showed us His humanity, and showed us how to Arise when tired and exhausted so that we may Thrive.

Challenge to Apply

The purpose of this devotional is to cause us to Arise under hardships and barren seasons so that we may Thrive. Thriving can only come through a relationship with our Heavenly Father. Every person on earth is unique, therefore everyone will have a unique relationship with the Father. But there are also foundations that we as Christians need, like prayer, study of the Word, community, etc. Take some time to evaluate how your connection with God is growing, and ask the Lord to reveal to you if you need to implement a new discipline of connecting with Him so that you may Thrive.

Stick it with Action

Let's follow in Jesus' footsteps tomorrow by rising early to spend time with our Creator. It doesn't have to be an hour earlier; maybe just 10 min earlier. Look at your calendar and see what tomorrow looks like. Then decide what time you will set your alarm and what time you will go to bed this evening. Ask the Lord for His strength and energy to Arise early to spend time with Him!

Praise God
DAY 5

Verse Challenge
Read Psalm 145. Pick a few verses from this Psalm to meditate on throughout the day.

I don't know about you, but sometimes I don't feel like praising God. Sometimes life is hard. Sometimes it's bleak. However, what I have learned throughout my time on earth, is that when it feels the most hopeless is when God's presence can break through in the brightest flash of hope.

In some of my lowest experiences, I chose and forced myself to thank God for little things throughout the day. And it was through Arising and turning my eyes upward, that I experienced to the greatest degree that the joy of the Lord is my strength.

This past week we've laid a foundation for pursuing a life that's lived to the full through Christ. This life needs to be built on the foundational truth that God is Good, that He Delights in you, that He's created you to live life to the full and that in order to do that we need to be connected to God.

Thriving in the barren places, or whatever season we find ourselves in, starts by Arising and praising God. It comes through remembering the goodness of God in the past and believing for that in the future.

Challenge to Apply

Take some time to write a list, a creative expression or prayer expressing thanks to God for how Good He is.

Stick it with Action

We often think of praise as an individual thing, yet in Scripture, particularly the Psalms, it was a corporate thing. You read of David stating that he will declare to the assembly the greatness of God. So today, be like David the worshipper, and tell someone how Good God is! Tell them what you're thankful to God for and why. Not only will this boost your experience of His joy, but your testimony will also uplift and strengthen those who hear!

Created Good

WEEK 2

DAY 6
Created Good

Verse Challenge

Read Psalm 139:13-15 slowly, and ask the Holy Spirit to highlight some specifics about how He created you.

This is a passage that many of us know if you've grown up in the church. In fact, I went to a Christian elementary school where we memorized these verses, but to be honest, it was just words. I didn't think much about what we were saying or the significance of it. Sometimes they are still just words that I 'know,' but haven't gone deep.

One fall, I joined a mom's group at my church, and one of the studies offered was 'Breaking Free from Body Shame' by Jess Connelly. I remember thinking 'What will people think if I join that class as a fitness coach?'

'Will people think that I struggle with body shame?' Yet, the other studies offered didn't intrigue me, so I went. And I'm so glad I did because the premise of the book was gold.

As women, we so often look at ourselves and shame our bodies. We see the imperfections, we treat it like a prize or a constant project, and often we just don't like it. Then you add on having kids, and it seems to all be accentuated! The overarching challenge of this book, however, was to agree with the Truth of God that our bodies have been created good. Period.

God does not make junk. He took time in creating us. He is the wise Creator who created you for a purpose. And that includes your physical body. He looks at you and He sees a masterpiece. Therefore, what must it do to the Father's heart when He hears us complain, compare and treat our bodies with contempt?

What kind of bondage is this body shaming putting us and the next generation in? Instead, what if we could actually agree with God about the fact that our bodies are created good... What kind of freedom might we find?

Challenge to Apply

We will continue to talk about the intricacies and hard questions regarding our bodies being created Good, but for now, take some time to write out or read the passage again slowly. Take some time think about how God knit YOUR body together. Stop and praise Him for the GOOD body He has given you. Ask the Holy Spirit to solidify truth in your heart and give you the courage to live in that truth moving forward.

Stick it with Action

Many times it's in the mirror that we start on a self-loathing, downward spiral. Today, go and clean your bathroom mirror. As you clean it, ask the Lord to give you a glimpse of how He sees you. Further, as you wipe away the spots and dirt, let it be symbolic of a new, clean start in your thinking to agree with how God has created you - that you are GOOD!

Created Holistically
DAY 7

Verse Challenge

Read 1 Kings 19:1-18. List the different emotions and states of mind that Elijah was in throughout this chapter.

When we read Scripture, it can sometimes be hard to put ourselves in the shoes of Biblical characters. Elijah was one of the greatest prophets in the Old Testament. He performed incredible signs and was a bold spokesperson against evil in Israel. But that doesn't mean he wasn't human or didn't experience many of the same struggles and emotions that we do.

In chapter 18, Elijah experienced a major high defeating 850 prophets of Baal and Asherah. Then he went to the mountaintop to pray and ask the Lord to end the drought. He must've been there for a while because he sent his servant seven times to look on the horizon to see if there were any clouds. Then on the seventh time, there was a speck in the distance which brought the rain. After these massive victories in the spiritual realm which affected the physical realm, Elijah heard that Jezebel wanted to kill him. And what's his response? A normal one of fear (verse 3).

Elijah fled, and we read that he laid down under a tree then asked to die (verse 4). What we find, however, is that he fell asleep only to be awaken by an angel to eat. This happens two times. In verse 7, we read that the angel was sent to give food and sleep to Elijah because he needed strength for the journey.

Last week we looked at the need for connection with God. Jesus, even though He was God, still carved out time to be with the Father. In the chapter before our passage today, you can read about Elijah doing great things in the Lord. After his experience in chapter 19, He went on a journey to encounter God on the mountain where he is encouraged and strengthened spiritually, but what did he require for that journey? Physical rest and food.

I believe more now than ever, that we are spiritual beings in physical bodies and in order to be Arise and Thrive, we need to cultivate health both spiritually and physically.

We need to Arise and connect with our Heavenly Father through worship, prayer, Scripture etc, but Thriving comes when we pair spiritual health with caring for our physical well being. The health of our physical bodies affects every other aspect of health - spiritually, mentally, emotionally, vocationally, relationally. When we're tired physically, depression has more potential to set in. When we're unhealthy physically, our stamina goes down. When we're not eating to fuel our bodies, we don't have the energy to carry out the mission God has called us to.

Challenge to Apply

Over our journey the next few weeks, we'll take time to focus on how to start planting seeds in the barren seasons of life to foster health spiritually and physically. For now, take some time to reflect on Elijah's experience - write down any ways that his journey may resonate with you. What do you think you might need from the Lord to carry on in vitality? Ask God for what you need today.

Stick it with Action

Do you have a time of day that you start to drag? Mine is mid to late-afternoon. Since we're holistic beings and our physical well-being affects other aspects of our being, try doing 10 squats, 10 lunges and 30 seconds of a wall sits the next time you start to drag. Take note and see if you notice any changes in your demeanour. Remember this experience and choose to Arise to do what you don't want so that you can actually Thrive and do what you do want.

Verse Challenge

Read Genesis 3 and take some time to write out the ways you have experienced the curse in your life.

It may feel weird to come back and talk about the effects of sin when we declared on Monday that we are created Good. Yet, when you follow the sequence of events in Genesis 1-2, we read that God's creation was good. We read that we were created for connection with Him and each other, and it was good. We read that we were meant to live forever in these physical bodies. But then everything goes south in chapter 3.

This can be our experience in our journey to Arise and Thrive - we can claim the truths of creation, only to have the effects of sin follow closely behind and waiver us in our belief that God is good and that we are created good.

The reality is that sin marred every aspect of our lives. No longer is a relationship with God or others perfect, instead we're estranged from God and others. Physically we live in the shadow of the curse carrying the effects of sin in our bodies from ailments, to physical disabilities, to gluttony, to old age, to death. But these do not negate the original intent of God creating mankind in His image, nor the declaration that our bodies are good.

Conversely, the entrance of sin brought about God's promise of a Deliverer who would strike the serpent's head and make a way back to Himself for His people; the fulfillment being Jesus.

Today we live in the 'Already / Not Yet' era. Through Jesus' death and resurrection, we have the ability to enter into a right relationship with God leading to spiritual health and Thriving! We have the ability to claim healing through Jesus' blood and restoration to the original word God spoke about our physical bodies - that they are Good! However, we also live in the 'Not Yet' because our physical bodies are slowly fading. So yes, they are created Good, but they aren't in their perfect form until Heaven.

The question is then, how do we Arise and Thrive in the here and now; in the face of the effects of sin? First, we need to identify the cause of sin. Are we experiencing sin's consequences because we live in a sinful world and sickness has marred God's good creation in our bodies? Or are we reaping the consequences of sinful habits we've formed?

Second, when we identify the root of sin, we need to decide what we will do moving forward. We can't change the past, but we can change how we approach the future. If we find out about sickness in our bodies, we can't change that fact, but we do have the opportunity to intercede and pray for healing in Jesus' name as well as do everything we can to rid our bodies of that sickness.

But what if we have sinful habits that will cause fallout in our holistic health - are we willing to radically make preventative changes in order to Thrive, or do we wait until the consequences of our actions hurt enough to make a change?

Part of deciding to move forward into Thriving in this 'Already / Not Yet' era is through changing our thoughts to align with the truth of God. We may know that God created our bodies good, but sometimes it feels impossible to declare. It may feel impossible, but when we don't agree with, believe or declare the truth of God that our bodies are good, it leads to bondage, just like Eve in the beginning. She didn't believe or declare the truth of God in the face of lies, and it led to bondage.

If we are serious about wanting to Arise and Thrive as God intended for us, a foundational part of starting a holistic health journey needs to be from the truth that God is Good and He created you good, despite the effects of sin. From there, freedom can be experienced which can propel you into living life to the full.

Challenge to Apply

Go back to what you wrote at the start of today in regards to the ways you've experienced the effects of sin in your life. Take some time to lay them before the Lord. Ask God to give you the desire, strength, courage and hope to pursue holistic health so that you may Thrive as He's created you to.

Stick it with Action

Does anyone else's purse or wallet become a holder for a bunch of unnecessary junk? This can be indicative of our lives too - carrying around junk that weighs us down. Take some time today to clean out your purse or wallet. Let it be an action that signifies how you're renouncing unhealthy habits that are weighing you down to start a new journey into health and Thriving.

Verse Challenge

Read Psalm 51 and write down the progression you see in David's prayer.

DAY 9

Repentance

Have you ever reached a point in your life where you're fed up and need to make a change? Or maybe you've done something that you knew was wrong and were broken in repentance.

When I was 21, I felt called by God to learn about fasting and to fast specifically for marriages once a week. It was a hard discipline, but so worth it in so many ways. However, one of the big insecurities in my life at that point was that I was single. It was hard that God asked me to pray for marriages when I wasn't even married. It felt like there was this heightened attack on me that year regarding my singleness, body-image and self-control.

I found myself binge eating and then going for longer runs the following day out of guilt. This cycle went on and on, with shame hanging over me along with self-loathing for my lack of control. Finally I broke. I was chatting with my parents on the phone, when I started to cry and asked them to pray for me because the weight of this cycle was too much.

I look back to that moment, as the moment in which that struggle's power weakened. I didn't realize it at the moment, as it was a slow process out of those habits, but over time I see the weight of sin, shame and poor habits lifting in that moment.

This week in our journey, we've started to look at how we're spiritual beings in a physical body. We've looked at how God created our bodies good and how our physical health affects other aspects of holistic health. We've also acknowledged that sin has marred God's original word of our bodies being good. Before we continue on to talk about taking care of our physical health as worship to carry out God's will, we need to camp in this passage.

Psalm 51 is a well-known Psalm written by David. The context of the writing was when he was confronted by the prophet Nathan about his adultery with Bathsheba. David's response was contrite, asking the Lord for forgiveness and cleansing so that he might be used again for God's purposes.

In this Psalm, David pleads, asking God to cleanse him. He declares in verse 4, 'Against you, you only, have I sinned.' What if we took all sin as seriously as this? Because the reality is that self-loathing, gluttony or self-harm is the same as adultery in God's eyes - they all separate us from our Creator.

What I love about this passage is that it doesn't stay in repentance or grief, but rather David moves to what he will do when he's forgiven, cleansed and restored. David states that he will teach transgressors and sinners; that he will sing of God's righteousness and declare His praise.

The beauty about this life is that failures and hardships are not wasted. Rather, they are opportunities to experience God's love and grace, as well as opportunities to share and teach others. But it starts with repentance.

Challenge to Apply

Take some time to sit in God's presence and ask Him to reveal "any wicked way in you" (Psalm 139:24) that you may need to repent of. Then take some time to reflect on how you treat your body - in thoughts, words and actions. If there is anything that doesn't line up with God's truth about how you're created good, ask the Lord to forgive you, and write a corresponding truth to the lie or sin against your body that you've been thinking, saying or doing. As you do the hard work to Arise through repentance, you'll slowly start to Thrive as God created you to.

_____

Stick it with Action

The one cupboard that drives me crazy in our kitchen is the one under the sink! It always seems to be nasty, and even though I open it multiple times a day, I choose to ignore it rather than clean it. As we're opening some hard, heart 'cupboards' to address this week, let's also take some time to address our kitchen cupboard as an action that says to ourselves we are not afraid to Arise, to address, or to do hard things so that we may Thrive.

_____

Celebration
DAY 10
Verse Challenge

Read Psalm 8 and take some time to praise God for how He has created us and who He is.

I grew up on the prairies in a rural area where you can see the sky without interruption. I love sunsets, sunrises, thunderstorms, northern lights and the stars at night with no light pollution! I love to look at the stars and contemplate how God created each of them with care, yet He sees me and delights in me! This humbling thought envelopes me as a warm hug. God sees me and knows me. He created me good. He created me with more thought than the stars - as we are the crowning jewel of creation!

This week we looked at the Truth that God created us good, but today we are going to declare it. It may feel awkward at first, but change often comes from rerouting neural pathways. Change doesn't come from emotions, but rather from declaring truth before we feel it, and as we declare truth consistently, it changes us until we feel it!

Let us ask the Lord to help us change our mode of operation from self-loathing to celebration of the bodies He has given us. Let us ask Him to help us Arise in transforming our eating habits and physical activity from a place of misuse to a sacred place of worship as we care for our bodies so that we may Thrive.

Challenge to Apply

Take some time today to evaluate your physical body and health from the lense that your body is good. Make a list of attributes that you like about your body. What are things that your body has accomplished that you're proud of or aspects of your body that you like?

Stick it with Action

After making your list, take some time to ask God for the truth about how you're created and then put that in different places around your house to remind you - on the mirror, at your sink, on your steering wheel, in your pantry, on your phone background - wherever! Now start to declare these truths and the things that you like or are proud of regarding your body when you catch yourself saying lies about your body.

Created for a Purpose

WEEK 3

Wisdom
DAY 11

Anyone else err on the side of being a control freak? I do! There are some great qualities that come alongside being a control freak, but there are also aspects that can alienate us from others. Alienation can then causes us to miss out on the benefits of community where the sum is greater than the individual parts.

I know how important it is to have people in my life or to work together to accomplish something, yet I still get sucked into my tendency to do it myself because it'll be done the way I like it. This same attitude can seep into how I live my life, thinking I know what's best.

Isn't it the case that we often go through life trying to figure it out ourselves? Even when reading the Bible it can seem like it doesn't apply to certain situations so we don't go to Scripture for wisdom.

That kind of thinking is really a lack of faith. When we look for step by step rules to follow it reveals an aspect of control within us. Rather, God says that we must live by faith. Therefore, we need to come to Him, the all-knowing Creator, who will guide us into wisdom and how to live in specific situations.

Wisdom has been a topic of discussion and something longed for throughout the ages. But what is Wisdom?

Wisdom is the practical application of Truth. The main focus being 'action.' It is greatly different from knowledge, in that knowledge can lead to thinking we know best, but wisdom, on the other hand, guides and informs us on how to live well and what that looks like practically.

So where and how do we get wisdom? It looks like where we started this journey in Week One with foundational truths - we get wisdom through connection with God.

When it comes to Almighty God, we read in Scripture that God is the Creator of all things. His power is seen through creation. Further, because He created all things, He is all-knowing; He knows how this world works because He put it together. Therefore, in order to obtain wisdom, we need to go to the Creator to understand how to live this life well. The practical application of how to live life well comes from a relationship with the Father!

Thriving and holistic health starts in a relationship with God. From that relationship, He leads us into wisdom - the practical application of truth. He will show us how to care for our bodies, how to invest in relationships, what our purpose is and how to renew our minds to take action. It starts in relationship to God.

Challenge to Apply

What situations are you facing now that you need wisdom for? Ask the Lord to speak to you, give you insight and power to walk in wisdom. If action is required, ask for His strength to Arise to the challenge before you. Invite Him into the process so that you may truly Thrive as you were created to.

Stick it with Action

Have you ever had a situation where you just don't know what to do, then someone with an outside perspective asks a question and it brings a light bulb moment? That's what God can do, and what we want to ask for today - an outside perspective. Take some time to tackle a closet that needs cleaning out; a closet that holds too much stuff that you 'should' keep but aren't sure why you're keeping. As you go through the items in there, ask yourself 'why do I have this?' Then move to asking, if you'll keep it, but rephrase the question to 'are you keeping it because you feel like you 'should' (guilt based) or 'want to keep it' (brings joy). If you're keeping something because you 'should' due to someone giving it to you, but you never use it, it is taking up mental space and not adding to the ability to Thrive, so put it in the pile to give away. (Throughout this process, take note how you feel when you allow yourself to release these things.)

Verse Challenge
Read Ecclesiastes 3:1-13. Write what this passage means to you.

Meaning
DAY 12

I was asked to speak at a high school's 'Spiritual Emphasis Week' one year, which I was very excited about until the coordinator asked me to speak on Ecclesiastes. All of a sudden, I was a bit overwhelmed.

Ecclesiastes starts with the words, "Meaningless, meaningless, everything is meaningless." How do you present something encouraging and passionate for teenagers from that? However, as I started reading and studying the book, I came to love it more and more.

Ecclesiastes is considered a wisdom book, therefore, there must be wisdom in it. However, it's not straightforward like the book of Proverbs. The premise of Ecclesiastes is that the author has tried everything in life seeking happiness and fulfillment, but realizes nothing fills the void. Nothing satisfies.

Then you come to the seemingly contradictory verse 3:13, in which the author states that work and enjoyment in life is a gift of God. The point is, everything we do is meaningless, but when God enters the scene, meaning and fulfillment come.

Over the past couple weeks, we've been creating a foundation of truth regarding how we're made as spiritual beings in a physical body that is good. Moving forward we will start to dig a bit deeper into what a health journey may entail with the desire to ultimately Thrive, but with that, there can be a nagging thought that holds us back. Even though Christians don't necessarily outright say that the physical is bad, we can focus so much on the spiritual where it can seem like putting any effort into our physical well-being can be 'bad' in comparison. Yet, I cannot align with this concept. If God created our physical bodies and declared them good, how can taking care of them be bad? If God gave us a physical body to serve and glorify Him with, how can nourishing it be bad? If God also states that our bodies will rise when Christ comes back and we'll get new, imperishable bodies, how can our physical bodies be bad?

The temptation as human beings is to make objects or areas of life our all-consuming focus. This can be a subtle shift when it comes to focusing on our physical health. However, caring for our bodies is of utmost importance if we are going to Thrive as God created us to. This is where its critical that we don't embark on a holistic health journey without God. It's imperative that we invite God into the process, because without Him, the journey is futile and meaningless. But with Him, strength to Arise comes and the ability to Thrive!

Challenge to Apply

Take time to be honest with yourself and God about how you're spending the time you have in this season. Ask the Lord to bring fruit in the areas that feel meaningful. And in the areas that feel meaningless, ask the Lord to infuse those times with His presence so that even mundane tasks may become full of promise. When we Arise in these seemingly meaningless areas of life, fruit and Thriving start to bud.

Stick it with Action

I can get so locked into the tasks at hand that I can easily forget God's presence and desire to speak in those mundane, seemingly 'meaningless' tasks. Today when you go to do the dishes, take a couple moments before starting to invite God into the mundane. Ask Him to reveal the sacred moment this 'futile' job can be and ask Him to speak to you through it.

DAY 13
Creativity

Verse Challenge

Read Genesis 1:26-31. Think about creation and meditate on the beauty you have seen in nature.

Have you ever found yourself dumbfounded watching an artist at work? Or have you looked on Pintrest to find some fun ideas just to be discouraged by some people's creativity and expertise in comparison to your 'lack of creative bone'?

This is me... I used to be artsy when I was a kid, but somewhere along the line I lost it!

I remember saying this to someone at church one time, when they stopped me and told me that my creativity was expressed in my preaching. I had never stopped to think of it like that, and in that moment was humbled by the fact that we have all been given the ability to be creative because we were created in the image of God - who IS the Creator!

On Monday, we talked about how God is the wise king who created the world through Wisdom. Because He created this world, He holds the keys and insight on how to live this life well. Furthermore, if we have been created in God's image, who is the incredible Creator, maybe there's an element that blesses His heart when we walk in creativity? In fact, I'm sure there is! He commissioned us to be His vice-regents on earth, to rule and subdue it. We need to be creative in order to rule as He has commissioned us to.

When we rule and exercise our creative side, we in essence breathe new life into areas that may have been stale, dead or 'formless and void.' Creativity does not need to mean writing poetry, painting or playing music (although it can). It transcends 'artistic boundaries' and is supposed to be used in all areas of life - relationships, work, parenting, Scripture reading, etc.

However, let's not be naive - creativity is not all rainbows and sunshine. Creating can be hard! What I find to be difficult when it comes to breathing life into stale areas, is either starting to create or finishing a project. It's like writing a paper in college that you can't bring yourself to start, but once you do it flows. Or starting a home reno with gusto, only to have it sit for months without the finishing touches. It's in these situations that we we need to ask ourselves if we're rested .

In Genesis 1, God declared His creation was very good and then He rested. We know that later in Scripture God calls us to rest once a week as well. I struggle with rest because I don't enjoy it. However, what I've found is that without rest we end up just surviving rather than having the capacity to Thrive.

All of life oscillates between activity and rest, ebb and flow. Inhaling and exhaling, summer and winter, planting and harvest. If we are constantly trying to produce and be effective, we lose out on the creative juices, because we are not infinite like our Creator God. In order to gain perspective in life, we need rest. Rest is where we are infused with courage to stand up to lies, or boldness to carry on in a decision to change and pursue health holistically.

At times we know we need to just start doing something in a particular area of life, but that can feel daunting or we're not sure where to start. On the flip side, we can be so inspired with ideas and thoughts that we start something whole-heartedly, but when the motivation wanes, we never finish.

This is human nature, and this is where we need to remember who we are (God's vice-regents called to rule with creativity), and tap into our source of creativity - God. We need Him to help us either start a journey, or ask Him to help us to continue a journey in order to bring it to completion.

Challenge to Apply

The whole point of this devotional is to lay a foundation of holistic health in order to move us into action rather than just talking about it. Start with some reflection on ways that you express creativity in your life and thank God for the ability to be creative. Then take some time to bring before God areas of influence which need to be infused with creativity from above. Lay these areas before the Lord and ask God for insight, creativity and the will to either start or continue the journey. Now Arise to action - choose a start day or make a plan to finish something that you started and haven't completed. Creating requires us to Arise, and when we start creating is when we start Thriving!

Stick it with Action

One of the hardest things these days is slowing down. So take a bath or something that forces you to slow down today or this week. During that time, just be. Don't feel like you have to evaluate or ponder or think about the to-do list. Rather just enjoy and rest. If you find that the to-do list is constantly on your mind, give those things to the Lord one by one.

DAY 14

Verse Challenge

Read Galatians 5:1. Why did Jesus come and how is that being lived out in your life?

_____

I love movies! I seriously just enjoy a good movie! One classic is Braveheart. Even though it's quite gory, it's incredibly well done. I love the heart-wrenching scene at the end when William Wallace screams out with his dying breath, 'FREEDOM!' All that he lived for, he stood by even in death. In a greater way, that's exactly what Jesus did! He came to give FREEDOM! He lived and died a gruesome death so that we may be free from the effects of sin, and so that we can live life to the full, starting today. We are saved, but how many of us are actually living free?

This week we've been building on the foundation of God's goodness and His declaration that we are created good. Upon this foundation, we want to move towards shifting our perspective through the renewing our minds regarding the barren season we may find ourselves in. Our thoughts are more powerful than we like to think, and they may be keeping us in the bondage for which Christ died to set us free. 2 Corinthians 10:3-5 says that we've been given divine power to destroy strongholds; power to destroy arguments and opinions that aren't in alignment with Christ. This divine power gives us strength to bring thoughts into obedience to Christ.

In our passage today, Paul was talking to Christians who were starting to doubt if Jesus' sacrifice was enough. There were false teachers telling them that they had to obey the Jewish law as an add-on to Christ's sacrifice. They had started to be burdened by the requirements of the law. So Paul states that they do not need to be weighed down by the law anymore, but rather they are free because of the Spirit. Jesus' sacrifice was enough to bring full freedom, nothing needed to be added to it, they just needed to accept it and live it out.

How often do we forsake the freedom that Jesus has purchased for us? We may think we're free, but the thoughts we think and tell ourselves may actually be contrary to what Christ says, and may be keeping us in bondage.

One way that I see Christians in bondage, is when we live life dictated by emotions. We start to wonder if God really loves us, or if God is even there. We wonder if He's good, or if He hears us. These thoughts are contrary to what Scripture says. It is of utmost importance to get into Scripture and let it transform us. We need to know the truth, because the truth sets us free (John 8:32). The kingdom of God is a life of faith. One passage says that we don't live by sight but rather faith. I like to say that we walk by truth not feelings. Emotions are fleeting and deceptive, but truth will set us free.

Let's go a bit deeper. In regards to your holistic health, which inner voice is winning out - emotions or truth? If we truly want to work on our physical health, yet keep choosing to sleep in or emotionally eat or skip the workout - we are constantly choosing to live by emotions. This is a slow 'death' in a sense. The fallout is not immediate, but rather a slow process which produces an outcome that will be less than Thriving; in fact it will be bondage instead of freedom.

Challenge to Apply

In order to take captive every thought we need to not only know the truth but actually live by the truth. Take some time and ask God to reveal to you how you may be living by emotions rather than truth. Then take some time to lay those situations before the Lord and ask for wisdom and His divine power to Arise over your emotions and do the hard things so that Thriving may come.

Stick it with Action

I grew up in Saskatchewan, and one of my favourite things to do in the summer is just drive on back roads with the windows down! There's something invigorating about it. As we've talked about freedom today, take a drive today with your windows down (even if it's winter - crank the heat and crack that window!) Enjoy the freedom of the wind in your hair, breathe in deeply the fresh air, and get excited for the ongoing freedom that you're Arising to step into.

Verse Challenge

Read Romans 12:1-2 and focus on verse 2 - what does it mean and what does it look like practically to be transformed?

DAY 15
Renew Your Mind

Motivation is a word that is constantly thrown around these days. The self-help industry is built on the notion of motivating others. In regards to spiritual health or fitness, I've often heard people say, they don't have motivation or that they're waiting for motivation. As I've worked with people and have continued to hear this, I've come to realize that motivation is not what we need in this life. Yes, motivation can be a great aid in kickstarting a habit. Yet, the reality is that motivation fades, so lasting change will not happen due to motivation. What do we need then if it's not motivation?

We need to make a decision; we need to put a stake in the ground and commit to act on what is decided.

That is what's needed.

One main purpose of this devotional, is not necessarily to make us feel good, but rather to push us to Arise under hardship, or to turn barren places into seasons of planting and watering. To position waiting times into times of growth and development. Yet, change is one of the hardest things we attempt to do in life.

Next week, we'll look more closely at this passage in its basic form of offering our physical bodies as sacrifices by taking care of our physical health. Yet, if you're like most people, the thought of starting a fitness journey is daunting and overwhelming. Aversion to change, growth or trying new things plagues all of us. We crave comfort and ease, but those are the very things that can lull us into barren places, void of life or Thriving. So how do we change? I believe the answer is found in this passage.

The way we change starts in the mind. If you listen at all to Joyce Meyers, you know that her big thing is 'the battle of the mind.' Why is the mind so important? Because what we dwell on or think about, becomes actions, actions dictate direction, and direction dictates where we end up. When you look through Scripture, you see that our thoughts are incredibly important. In verse 2, we're instructed to be transformed by the renewing of our mind because that's how we'll be able to test and discern (ie. have wisdom) how to live life well.

What does it look like to renew our minds and thoughts? It looks like diving into Scripture, to be washed by the water through the Word (Ephesians 5:26). It looks like agreeing with the truth about what God says about you. It looks like dwelling on things above, not below (Colossians 3:1-2). It looks like meditating on what's upright (Philippians 4:8).

Basically, renewing our minds takes discipline. Renewing our minds means creating new thought pathways. It means being stronger than our emotions. It looks like declaring the truths from Weeks 1-2 even when we don't feel like it.

Challenge to Apply

Take some time to evaluate where you need to change your thoughts and renew them to agree with God's truth. Are there any areas of health that you've been waiting for motivation, when really you just need to make a decision to commit? Ask God to help you Arise in the face of hardship to stick to your commitment, so that you may turn your barren season into one of Thriving.

Stick it with Action

The mind is so powerful, and what we fill it with is what will come out. Instead of being passive about what goes in, let's take initiative and fill our minds with truth. Take some time to either write out or print out Romans 12:1-2 and put it in various places around your house (the mirror, shower, above the toilet paper dispenser, in the pantry, by your kitchen sink, etc) to prompt you to continue to make healthy habits as well as to help you memorize this passage of Scripture.

Created to Grow

WEEK 4

Growth
DAY 16

Verse Challenge

Read 1 Timothy 4:11-16 and write what Timothy was charged to do and why.

Everyone says it, but having kids really does change your life. It's incredible to watch these little humans grow and develop before your eyes. To see the determination to walk, or focus required to put a train track together, and then to see them talking and actually conversing with you is astounding!

Babies and toddlers change so fast, and you see the changes almost daily as they're growing. In contrast, adults seem to struggle to change, even good change. However, when I read what Paul writes to Timothy, it seems like adults are never supposed to stop changing and growing.

Paul exhorts Timothy to continue to walk in righteousness, and to not get comfortable with where he's at. Rather, he's to continue to push himself to develop his gifts. Timothy is told to 'practice,' 'immerse,' and 'keep a close watch.' These are all focused action words that require discipline. In turn, these actions would produce fruit as people would see progress in him. I'm sure at times Timothy didn't want to be diligent in discipline, but what was on the line was too important and therefore, the option to stay stagnant wasn't viable. Paul told Timothy to be diligent in these things because people's salvation depended on it.

Maybe you don't feel like the stakes are so high for you, but what if they are and you don't realize it? The point is not to evaluate your impact on others, but rather to consider how you're growing. It may be a barren, waiting season, but that doesn't mean that it's not a season for planting. Just because you're saved, doesn't mean you've arrived. Rather, we're called to do hard things. We're called to continue to grow. There's supposed to be progress seen in our lives, but it requires discipline.

Challenge to Apply

Take some time to lay before the Lord your health. Ask Him to reveal some actions you can start taking to continue your decision to grow in holistic health. Then ask the Holy Spirit to empower you to Arise from inaction to actually take steps towards health, because only then will we start to grow and Thrive.

Stick it with Action

In Canada we have quite distinct seasons and there's nothing quite like the anticipation of spring when all that has 'died' comes back to life! The haze of green in the trees before the leaves pop, the tiny green points that start to sprout up in the grass, and the sweet song of the birds in the morning!
As we talked about growth today, get some seeds for a flower that you'd like to plant. Let it be a reminder to you for your the areas of life that you are planting in and let it spur you to continue to Arise to plant in the seasons you're in.

DAY 17
Unstoppable

Verse Challenge

Read Philippians 4:10-13. What have you always thought this passage means? What might it actually be saying?

When I used to work at camp, we'd help campers memorize scripture. It felt like something we would recite to cross off the list and forget ten seconds later. That mentality irritated me because I wanted these campers to go home with the Truth hidden in their heart. So we started making fun rhythms, voices and beats to which we could memorize the verses. Fifteen years later, many of those verse are still engraved in my head, one of them being Philippians 4:13.

I think there are many Christians who love this verse. It's powerful and hopeful, but we don't often consider the context. Paul is sharing the secret of contentment. He states that whether he's rich or poor, hungry or full, he knows he can face any situation because the Lord strengthens him.

In today's North American Christianity, there's this thought that Christians shouldn't have to suffer or face hardships. Even if we know the passages about persecution, we are still often distraught when hardships come our way.

Obviously emotions will come up when we're facing situations that are difficult, but do we have peace like Paul states earlier in verse 6? Do we have contentment because we know we're not alone in that situation? Do we walk forward in confidence knowing that there's another in the fire with us?

The point is that we are called to do hard things, but we don't have to do them by ourselves. Jesus said that we will have trouble, but that He has overcome the world. He said that the one who is in us is greater than the one who is in the world. He has given us Himself as a sacrifice, and His Spirit as a guide and comfort to empower us when facing hard times.

Challenge to Apply

What situations are you facing that you need to declare that you can do all things through Christ? Take some time to list those and invite the Holy Spirit to empower you in these situations. After inviting Him, thank Him and ask for the peace that surpasses understanding and His contentment for today so that you may Arise above the hardship into Thriving.

Stick it with Action

To remind yourself that you can do hard things in the power of the Spirit, get outside and do some work. Maybe that means shovelling the walkways, or doing some work in the garden, or maybe even just going for a run. But take some time to get out and work. While you work invite the Holy Spirit to strengthen you from your inside out so that you may face the challenges ahead with His power and peace.

Strength

Verse Challenge

Read 2 Peter 1:3-11. Notice what God has given us, and then note what we're called to do.

Have you ever been given a task to do at work yet weren't given the appropriate authority? Or have you tried to tackle a project at home without the correct tools? It's basically a recipe for disaster. You can still accomplish what you were commissioned or set out to do, but it doesn't come without a lot of frustration and piecemeal parts.

Thankfully God does not do that. Instead when He calls us to do something, He equips us with the right tools. In fact, this passage says that He has given us everything for life and godliness. This seems a bit exaggerated because at times, life just seems unfair. Sometimes it feels like we're in groundhog day not moving anywhere. Sometimes we're in a barren season with no signs of growth or vitality. Sometimes godliness seems so far off because we continually mess up, which leaves us wondering if we'll ever grow in godliness. It's in these times that we need to come back to the truth of God's Word, because He says that He's given us EVERYTHING for life and godliness.

Now, don't get me wrong. The fact that God has given us everything, doesn't mean that He'll do the work for us. Rather, it's a partnership. God has done everything for us on the Cross and in giving the Holy Spirit to us, but now He calls us to 'work out our salvation' as is stated in Philippians 2:12-13. Or in the rest of 2 Peter 1 we're exhorted to 'make every effort.' The implication of making every effort speaks to me that we actually have to work to grow in our salvation. This is the great tension between being cleansed and sanctified by God, but then working it out incrementally over the course of our lives.

The bottom line is that we are called to do hard things. We're called to make every effort. This is our part in response to God's all-encompassing action. So today, let's partner with the truth that God has given us everything we need to Arise and make 'every effort,' so that we may truly Thrive.

Challenge to Apply

What situations are you facing in which you need to declare the truth that God has given you everything for life and godliness? Take some time to list those and invite the Holy Spirit to empower you to Arise in these situations. After inviting Him, thank Him and ask Him to help you to Arise and make every effort in those areas so that you may Thrive and bring Him glory.

_____

Stick it with Action

We have become so distracted these days with entertainment and noise all around us. All the noise, however, can weaken our resolve or focus on what needs to be done, or what we desire to do, because we're numbed by everything around us. Decide to take a day in the next week to fast from social media, or from electronics, or to turn the music off so that you can just be and focus on what God is calling you to do. Ask for strength in this fast, and ask that the strength would flow into the areas of life you are pursuing change in.

Verse Challenge

Read Galatians 5:22-25. Highlight a few of the qualities listed where you see evidence of the Spirit producing fruit in you.

I love fruit! It's like nature's dessert for us to enjoy! I remember going to my grandparent's place in the Okanagan when I was young and coming home with boxes of fruit. Cherries that exploded in your mouth and such juicy peaches making it impossible to eat without the sweetness dripping down your chin! I always wished I lived in a climate that would produce fruit trees better, but I guess I'll just enjoy the memories.

I love how the Bible uses nature as analogies for spiritual truths. When we read about the Fruit of the Spirit, we tend to look at each individual aspect as if there were nine different fruit trees. However, the way Paul writes indicates that there is one tree and one fruit.

These nine characteristics are all part of the one fruit that the Holy Spirit produces in us. Some characteristics might be more noticeable than others, but God is in the process of developing His fruit in your life. How encouraging is that!

At times I've heard people use this passage as an evaluation tool to see where they're lacking and what they need to work on. This goes directly against the passage, since it's not our fruit produced by our efforts; rather it's the Holy Spirit's fruit that He cultivates in our lives.

So what's our part? It's to partner with the Holy Spirit. It's to ask Him to produce more of Himself in us. It's to spend time with God through prayer, worship, Scripture reading, etc. to prepare our heart's soil. It's to walk in freedom knowing that we do not have to try to earn our way to Heaven.

This week, we talked about doing hard things, and how Christ will empower us to face any situation so that we can be content. The day before that we talked about discipline and growth. Today I want to encourage you that whatever situations you're facing, or area of health that you want to grow in, that you don't have to do it alone!

Challenge to Apply

Take some time to ask the Holy Spirit to show you what fruit He's producing in you. Then ask Him what areas you need to surrender to Him more - is it to be loving, or patient, maybe self-controlled. Ask Him to help you to say no to things that lull you into a survival mode rather than Arising to do the hard things that bring about Thriving and ultimately God's glory.

Stick it with Action

As we have looked at our lives to see what fruit God is producing in our lives, let's do something to signify the desire the Spirit has to continue to produce His fruit in your life. Swing by a grocery store today and pick out one of your favourite fruits or one that is a treat. Take it home and share it with your family, or enjoy it by yourself and ask the Lord to continue His great work in you as you partner with Him to produce fruit in your life.

Time for Action
DAY 20

Verse Challenge

Read 1 Peter 1:13-16. How might this passage not only apply to spiritual disciplines but also living to pursue holistic health in God's power and for His glory?

As I've already shared, I love movies! But the movies I really enjoy aren't necessarily chick flicks (although I can find myself enthralled in those too). Instead, the genre that I love are war movies. I love watching the struggle and prevail of the hero in the face of battle. As you start to compare the characters in almost any war or action movie, it becomes apparent that each hero had to decide in their minds beforehand what must be done regardless of the sacrifice it might require.

In the same way, this passage is warning us that a battle is raging, and we need to prepare our minds. Later in Peter's book, he pulls back the curtain on what's going on behind the scenes. He points out that we have an enemy prowling around like a lion wanting to destroy us.

Peter warns and exhorts the church to prepare their minds for action. To dial it in and decide to live for God no matter what the cost. To settle in their minds how they must live in a dark world. Peter challenged them to set their hope on Jesus so that they might not be conformed to the world, but rather transformed into God's holy likeness.

Now first century Christians were facing horrific persecution under Nero the Emperor of Rome. In North America, we aren't facing persecution like that. But there is still a battle. The battle, however, is more subtle. Instead of physical persecution, a lot of the battle is to distract, lull us to sleep, or lead us into shame so we're left in bondage feeling useless for the Kingdom.

Today, I believe, is the day we need to take a stand and prepare for action. We've spent the past four weeks building a foundation of truth about Who God is, who we are, and how we're created for connection with Him so that we may Thrive. Further, we've laid a foundation of the fact that we are spiritual beings in a physical body and how Thriving requires some hard work to Arise out of where we find ourselves; it requires pursuing holistic health so that we can glorify God. We've laid this foundation, and hopefully your mind is now ready for action so that we can  actually start changing our routines and thoughts to produce healthy habits. From new habits that we create, our stamina will increase, enabling us to step into our God-given role as vice-regent and co-creator as we breathe life into formless areas around us.

Next week will be starting to look at tangible ways of pursuing health, followed by a couple weeks evaluating where we're at and creating goals to focus us toward action, so that we might truly Arise and Thrive.

Challenge to Apply

Take some time to look back at the past 4 weeks. What have been some profound moments that you have had with the Lord? What is your perspective in regards to making changes - are you hopeless, hesitant, hopeful or excited? Write down where you're at and ask the Lord to empower you and lead you to the next area so that you may have the ability to Arise under whatever you're facing and Thrive for God's glory.

Challenge to Apply

As we talked about arming our minds for action and deciding to move forward into action and change, I want us to do something physical that signifies a change in our life; today we are going to put a stake in the ground - literally!
I want you to find a piece of wood, or lath, or even popsicle stick that is going to be a marker of new life. Take this stick and either write on it what you want this new season to look like, or key words that you want this season to be defined by. Then as you take that stick and drive it in a flower bed, or a potted plant say the words, 'It's time to Arise and Thrive!'

Created to Arise

WEEK 5

Life of Worship

DAY 21

Verse Challenge

Read through Romans 12:1-2 slowly a few times and write down what worship looks like.

Last week we ended by putting a stake in the ground to Arise by changing habits so that we may Thrive. This week is action mode. We're going to get moving on some of the areas of health that we've laid a foundation for, and start actually doing something about those areas.

We looked at this passage on Day 15 and how renewing our minds requires filling it with truth, but I want to back up a bit and ask, what does Paul mean when he says 'offer your bodies as living sacrifices?' What would it look like if we took this command at its most basic level and acted in obedience? And what is the basic command? I think part of it is taking care of our physical bodies through fitness, nutrition, and rest as an act of worship to God.

As I've mentioned before, in the church we tend to focus so much on spiritual health because physical health doesn't seem 'spiritual.' However, since we are spiritual beings in a physical body, everything we do has a spiritual aspect to it, including our physical choices.

I spent 10 years in Pastoral Ministry, and looking back I realized that I talked so much about spiritual health without really connecting how caring for our physical health can affect our overall health. Looking back on my time in ministry, I wish I talked more to students about how worship and sacrifice can look like physical hygiene; it can look like moving our bodies to guard against anxiety; it can look like getting good sleep to guard against depression; it can look like caring for our bodies as the vessel we've been given to glorify God with rather than finding our worth in how we look; it can look like strengthening our bodies to walk in confidence; it can look like fuelling our bodies to feel good rather than eating junk or developing poor coping mechanisms with food (which tends to be acceptable in the Christian world because at least its not 'drugs or alcohol'). Worship is a posture of living which includes our physical health as much as our spiritual health.

With that being said, what if we cared for our physical bodies as worship rather than a means of punishment for binging? What if we asked for discipline to workout instead of waiting for motivation to start? What if we made healthy food choices not out of self-hatred, but out of thanksgiving for the body God has given us?

Paul used the phrase, 'offer your bodies as living sacrifices,' which we in our North American Culture, don't fully grasp. When Paul was writing this letter, people had a vivid understanding of the word 'sacrifice'. The Jews once a year would slaughter a lamb to pay for their sins, among the multiple other sacrifices they offered throughout the year. The thing about sacrifice is that there was a cost, and offering your body as a living sacrifice will be just that, a sacrifice.

In order to offer our bodies as living sacrifices, we will need to Arise out of the unhealthy habits we've formed, and in that struggle is where the sacrifice is found as well as God's presence and glory. The reality is that God has made our bodies good, and this is the body He's given us to worship and serve Him, not only in this life, but also throughout eternity, so let us start now by offering it as a sacrifice.

Challenge to Apply

Take some time and ask the Lord to show you what offering your body as a sacrifice might look like for you. Then evaluate what the outcome could be of offering your body as a living sacrifice. Ask the Lord to empower you to Arise to cut ties with uhealthy habits so that you may step into Thriving as you offer your body as a living sacrifice.

Stick it with Action

Many times we think that a fitness journey has to be all-encompassing, hard and unenjoyable. But that does not have to be the case! Fitness is supposed to add to your life, bring energy, a sense of accomplishment and joy. It also doesn't have to look traditional like getting to the gym and lifting weights (which many times can intimidate and overwhelm us because we don't know where to start).

So today, carve out 30min to do this dance workout! You will be sweating and working your body, but also laughing, having fun and allowing joy to come as you move your body.

XB Sweat and Sculpt - Dance Workout -
www.beachbodyondemand.com/programs/xb-sweat-and-sculpt/start-here?
referralprogramid=XBSS&referringrepid2395431=&trainername=AndreaRogers

Verse Challenge

Read Psalm 3:1-6 and write out how this passage comforts and challenges you.

When I was finishing High School and into my first few years of college, I worked at a Bible Camp. It was some of the most fulfilling summers of my life! We were outside, we were doing activities and adventures all day, and most of all we were sharing the Gospel with the youth who came for a week of camp. Over 8 weeks of campers though, you start to get a little weary - especially when you're going on 6 hrs of sleep each night and hard each day. I remember reading this passage one summer and verse 5 became a prayer throughout that season.

At that point, I never paid attention to what David was going through when he wrote this, but it's profound to know the back story. He wrote this Psalm during one of the lowest experiences in his life. This wasn't written at the beginning of his life before he was king, nor was it written during the height of his reign. Rather, this was written after he left Jerusalem because one of his sons had conspired against him and came to Jerusalem to dethrone him. David fled, and this is the Psalm that he wrote in that season (cf. 2 Samuel 15-18).

Can you imagine being in David's shoes? Having your own son not only go behind your back, but then run you from your home and your kingship, ultimately wanting to kill you? How does anyone cope with a situation like this? I think two keys in dealing with hard seasons of life are found in this verse.

Number one - David knew he was created for connection with God. So he pressed into the Lord and was communing with His Creator which strengthened his spirit.

Number two - he knew he needed sleep to deal with the situations that he faced.

Here's the thing. God is the one who gives sleep to those He loves (Psalm 127:2), but it's also a necessary discipline to get your sleep in order to deal with the situations that come up in life.

Again, we are spiritual beings in a physical body. We need to take care of our spiritual health through spiritual disciplines, but just as important is caring for our physical bodies through discipline. The effects that sleep has on our emotions, hormones, capacity to deal with hard situations, and how our bodies fight illness and injury is incredible. God started creating on the first day with time - evening and morning. Within a 24 hour period, half of it is night which was created for rest. Again, within a 7 day period, God set aside one day for rest. Further, in Jewish thought, the beginning of the new day was not when the sun came up, but rather when the sun went down, which one can argue that a good day starts with a good sleep.

We are holistic beings - spiritual beings in a physical body. Our physical bodies affects so many other aspects of our health and wellbeing, so how are you resting?

Challenge to Apply

What are you going through these days? What are you facing? Are you riddled with anxiety regarding situations, or are you able to sleep in peace? Take these situations to the Lord in prayer and ask Him to intervene and exchange your fear and anxiety for His peace. Then evaluate what your sleep schedule is like, and if it needs to change. Ask the Holy Spirit to give you discipline to get to bed, as well as ask for His gift of rest.

Stick it with Action

One thing that I love to do is read a Psalm before going to sleep. I found it calms my mind and focuses my thoughts on things above before I close my eyes. Tonight, instead of scrolling social media, grab your Bible and read a Psalm before you sleep.

Verse Challenge

Read Ephesians 4:17-24.
What is Paul calling the church to do in this passage?

Have you ever had something from your past haunt you in your dreams or flashbacks? Or have you had a situation that just seems to hang over everything even though you're trying to move forward? This is a similar situation that Paul is addressing.

In this passage, Paul instructed the Church to not live like Gentiles anymore. What we can gather from Paul's encouragement is that the Believers at that time were still in bondage to habits from before coming to Christ. These former habits were hindering them from living life to the full. Paul paints a picture describing how Gentiles live darkened in their understanding and that their hearts were hard. This hardness lead them into, what's translated in the NIV, as a 'continual lust for more'. Therefore, Paul exhorted the Ephesian Christians to put off habits that give into the desires of the flesh so that they may be renewed and live life to the full.

There are many acts and habits that lead to bondage that we as Believers set aside in order to live life to the full, but one that I have rarely heard any teaching on is our eating habits.

I was basically born in the church. Every Sunday growing up, we were in church. I went to a Christian High School and Bible College, as well as served at camp, in my teen and young adult years, all of which had multiple chapel services in a week. I've gone to countless conferences and Christian events. And through all of this, I can vividly remember two messages that talked about our eating habits. The reason I remember them, is because it's something never talked about. One was at church when I was in high school, and the other was in my thirties at a Leader's conference. Why is it that we don't talk about eating habits in church?

Something one speaker pointed out is that we like our 'potlucks.' In a sense, gluttony is assumed to be a lesser 'evil' than getting drunk or adultery, so we let it slide. Further, in my ministry and running events over the years, I know that snacks and food are elements that break down barriers to bring people together; there is something spiritual about gathering to eat together. Look at Scripture, all of the major events are celebrated with a party and a feast. Even when we get to Heaven, there is the anticipation of the wedding feast of the Lamb. So of course, the enemy would twist something that is good to become something that can cause bondage so we don't live life to the full.

Why does it matter? Well throughout my time in ministry I've witnessed a similar type of shame in women regarding their bodies and eating habits, as I've seen in men who struggle with pornography. It seems like women can get caught in the shame cycle of gluttony, and it paralyzes them. I've seen justification on one hand for their actions that leads to indulgence, but on the other hand an isolation from community, embarrassment, and sense of 'disqualification' from being used by God. Then, once in isolation, there's a deeper spiral indulging in the act that started the shame cycle in the first place. Jesus did not die so that we can just get to Heaven, yet struggle with shame throughout our lives.; He came to set us free so we can Thrive.

What if we believed that Jesus died to break us free from the bondage of gluttony and body-shame? What if we believed that He wants to journey with us into right thinking and wholeness in regards to our eating habits? What if we viewed how we eat as an opportunity to glorify God like we're instructed in Colossians 3:17 - "whatever you do, in word or deed, do everything in the name of the Lord Jesus, giving thanks to God the Father through Him." Maybe then hope would Arise and we would start to eat with intention to fuel our bodies and glorify God rather than satisfy bodily cravings that lead us into bondage.

If we are created to Thrive, yet the way we eat has us wrapped up in a shame cycle that leads to loathing the good body that God has created, then there might be an issue. We are created holistically, therefore how we eat really does affect not only our physical health, but also our spiritual health, which can lead to lies and spiritual bondage that doesn't align with God's truth about who we are.

Challenge to Apply

Maybe you don't struggle with over-eating, but maybe you do struggle with under-eating, or yo-yo dieting, or self-loathing of your physical appearance. Maybe you don't have issues with your eating habits, but maybe you're not aware of God's presence and the opportunity to worship Him in your eating. Take some time to evaluate how you care for your body through your eating habits, then invite God to give you wisdom and power to renew your mind so that you may Arise and fuel your body as an act of worship to God. As you Arise in this area, may Thriving start to seep in as we live as God intended.

Stick it with Action

One quote that I love is 'planning isn't half the battle, it is the battle.' This is what I've found with food and meals. It can feel rigid at times to meal plan, but when you plan out what you're going to make, eat and snack on throughout the day, it actually creates more space mentally, it helps with budgeting, as well as cuts down on over-indulging. Take some time today to plan your meals for 3 days of next week. Then decide what you need from the grocery store and schedule a time over the weekend to pick up the groceries you need.

DAY 24

Prepare for Victory

Verse Challenge

Read Luke 4:1-15. Notice the role of the Holy Spirit in this passage as well as Jesus' response to Satan's accusations.

Have you ever started something just to be stopped as soon as you started? It's like traveling with kids and the moment you're ready to go, one of them has to go to the bathroom (or maybe it's not a kid, but you!)

In life it is so frustrating when this happens. It can be disheartening when you're ready to move on something, act or change, and all of a sudden a distraction or situation comes up that derails you before you begin.

In this passage, Jesus had just been baptized and was probably feeling very good. It's interesting though, because then we read that He's led by the Holy Spirit into the desert to be tempted. Talk about a bit confusing and disheartening! Jesus had just heard the voice of the Father declaring Jesus as His Son and that the Father was pleased with Him. I'm sure Jesus wanted to start His mission then, but there was a necessary detour that needed to be made, and not an enjoyable one.

I would say situations like this happen often in life. We have an experience, or have mustered up courage to change and start a journey into Thriving, then all hell breaks loose. I don't think it's coincidence, but rather very strategic by the enemy to try to derail us before we gain momentum. Think about it, if you have decided to start a journey into Thriving, the enemy will want to stop it because he hates when we live life to the full. He hates when we Thrive because the glory of God is evident when we are fully alive.

Let's look at how the enemy attacked Jesus - he attacked Jesus' identity. Satan tried to plant doubt in who Jesus knew He was, followed by a temptation to do something in order to 'prove' Jesus' lordship. In the same way, the enemy attacks our identity and tries to lodge doubt in who we are. 'Who are you to change?' 'You're a nobody.' 'Why even start when you've tried before and just failed?' 'You're too far gone.' 'The road is too hard.' It is in the face of these lies that we need to cling to and declare God's truth.

Here's what I want us to end on and dwell on as we go throughout our day and week - that God is more powerful! Jesus is victorious! We need to be aware of and wise to the ploys of the enemy, but we don't need to dwell on them and dissect every little distraction claiming that it's an attack. Rather we need to focus on who Jesus is and the victory won at the cross! We need to remind ourselves that the One who lives in us is greater than the one in the world (1 John 4:4). We need to remember that the same power that raised Christ from the dead lives in us (Ephesians 1:19-20). We need to declare that we have been given everything for life and godliness (2 Peter 1:3).

God has created you to Thrive! Do not fear the distractions, temptations or failures, rather be ready and arm your mind with truth to dismantle the lies of the enemy. Then walk forward in confidence in the decision to Arise and Thrive!

Challenge to Apply

Have you experienced some distractions or temptations recently? How did you respond? How might you need to fight differently, or continue to prepare your mind and heart for battle? Ask the Lord for wisdom and strength to help you Arise in the face of distractions so that you may fully Thrive.

Stick it With Action

Today, we're going to practice and stick our victory with action through some self-talk. When I used to coach kids at camp on how to ski or wakeboard, I'd have them say loudly 'I can do it!' three times before trying. If they said it with confidence and gusto, a lot of the times they would get up!

There's power in our thoughts and words, so let's fill them with truth. Declare right now, out loud, three times, 'I'm a Daughter of the King!' Then follow it up with 'I'm victorious because Christ is victorious!' Repeat these lines throughout the day, and take note of your demeanour, attitude and how you handle situations!

Decide
DAY 25

Verse Challenge
Read Romans 15:4-6, 13 and take note of the words and themes that are repeated in these few verses.

Our culture talks a lot about self-care these days, because we try to live as infinite beings which can cause burnout. However, many times we confuse self-care with self-comfort. Self-comfort is nice in the moment, but it may actually keep us from what we ultimately need. In contrast, self-care at times can look like doing what's uncomfortable in order to achieve holistic health and goals down the road.

I know I don't usually feel like reading the Bible or going to church, but if I want to grow in my relationship with the Lord, I carve out time in order to hear from Him and get to know Him. I don't feel like working out or being self-disciplined in my eating, but I know I feel and have more energy if I'm disciplined in those areas.

It sometimes doesn't seem necessary to go through the hassle of getting a babysitter and going out for a date with my husband, but the fruit that it can produce is worth it. I never felt like doing homework or reading, but without discipline a Masters degree would have never happened.

Over the course of the month we have looked at who God is and how He created us for connection with Him. He has created us to live life to the full in order to honour and glorify Him. We've also looked at the fact that we are spiritual beings in physical bodies. To truly Thrive, we need to develop discipline through renewal of our minds so that we may be the best we can be, even if we're in a barren time.

What season are you in? Do you want to turn your barren seasons into ones of planting and watering rather than just waiting and surviving? Then I believe it requires discipline. Farmers know when it's time to work, and even in the waiting, they know growth is taking place because of the discipline they had in the planting. A lot of our life comes down to discipline. If we want to live life to the full to glorify God, there's an element of putting a stake in the ground, making a decision and being disciplined to structure our lives in order to grow.

I believe God desires you to Thrive! After this past month, I pray that your mind is ready for action and that today is the day that you make a decision to act rather than waiting for motivation. I pray that today is the day that you decide enough is enough. I pray that today is the day that you decide to Arise and Thrive!

Challenge to Apply

Take some time to write a prayer to God expressing your desire to Arise and Thrive in regards to your holistic health. Invite Him into the process. Ask for His help and discipline to Arise. End with writing out how you desire Him to be glorified as you decide to Thrive in your barren places.

Stick it With Action

The scary thing about change is the fear of failure. We don't want to start something just to quit and have people disappointed in us. This is a normal and natural fear. However, if we let the fear of failure or fear of man keep us from growth, then we aren't living life to the full. Further, we need people in our lives to cheer us on and hold us accountable when we're pursuing growth.

Call a trusted friend today and tell them the journey that you're on. Share with them the ways in which you are starting to pursue health. Tell them how you're ready to Arise to the challenge so that you may Thrive. Share with them how scared you are, but how you need them to cheer you on. Take some time after calling your person to journal how you felt during and after the call.

Created for Reflection
WEEK 6

Verse Challenge

Read Psalm 139:23-24 and ask the Lord to search your heart and thoughts during today and tomorrow in regards to your holistic health. Ask Him to encourage you where you need encouragement, convict you where you need conviction and boldness to be honest with yourself.

Congrats! You've made it this far! We spent five weeks working on developing a spiritual discipline of reading the Bible every day which has led you here! How do you feel? What have you learned? Remember those things, because that's how we keep going when we don't want to.

Further, we've spent the past five weeks looking at truth to align our hearts and mind with as it pertains to holistic health and Thriving. We've done some hard work of preparing our minds, but now it's time for action. Over the next few weeks, we will start a process of evaluation to see where we're at regarding our health and then put goals in place and establish action items that will lead us closer to living life to the full. So let's jump in.

Socrates said in the first century that "an unexamined life is not worth living." But as Believer's we don't just have to rely on our own ability to evaluate. Instead, we have the Power of God in the Holy Spirit indwelling us who will reveal things to us that we don't even know about ourselves. In order to continue to progress to Arise and Thrive as busy women, we need to take stock of our overall health.

If you read all of Psalm 139, you will see that God created and knows us to a degree we can't comprehend. We are finite beings, but He is infinite and knows everything there is to know about us. He knows us better than we know ourselves and sees the areas we're Thriving in and the areas that we're not. In the areas that we're not living life to the full, He wants to journey with us into Thriving, and the first step is evaluation.

Challenge to Apply

Take today and tomorrow to evaluate yourself and reflect on how you're doing as you work through the corresponding questions.

Start by rating yourself from 1-10 in the following areas:

- Spiritual Health (Connection and growth with God) _____

- Physical Health (Activity, nutrition and rest) _____

Describe Why you rated yourself the way you did in each area. What is contributing to health or lack of health in each area?

Now take some time to evaluate how each area is affecting the other area of health.

Which area of health would you like to focus on improving in the next month or 6 months? Is there a particular aspect of that area of health that you'd like to focus on (i.e. Prayer, or Service or Fasting for Spiritual Health; or Nutrition, or Rest or Cardio, or Mobility in Physical Health)?

Invite the Lord to be part of the process in the weeks and months to come so that you may live the life to the full, Thrive and glorify God.

Evaluation of Values
DAYS 28-29

Read Matthew 6:19-21. How may this passage inform how we pursue holistic health and the desire to live life to the full?

On Monday and Tuesday we took time to evaluate and reflect on how we're doing in our holistic health. Today and tomorrow I want to move us into deeper reflection of our health as we uncover the motives and values that affect how we spend our time, money and energy.

However, before we jump into the evaluation process, I want to ground ourselves in the passage we read today. Jesus told us to lay up for ourselves treasures in Heaven, and warned us that where our treasure is, that's where our heart will be. I want us to be aware of what our motives for holistic health are. It can be a slippery slope when pursuing physical health to slip into idolatry of one's body. Hopefully with our foundation work at the beginning of this devotional, we have our motives right, but I want to caution us to keep them right as we dive into action. The reason we want to Thrive needs to ultimately be for the experience of God's glory in our lives - that is the greatest thing and the only lasting motivation! Let us take a moment right now to invite God to be and remain our focus throughout this journey.

Values are a hot topic in today's society. It seems as though every business and church feels the need to identify and post their values.

But what are values? One definition states: "a person's principles or standards of behaviour; one's judgment of what is important in life." The reason it's helpful for entities to identify their values is to guide their decision-making.

For individuals, it's helpful to identify personal values as well in order to live in alignment to what's important. Values or priorities are exhibited in how we spend our time (our most valuable asset) and money (the currency we've assigned to show the value of something). Basically, values reveal where our energy goes and what energizes us.

There is a difference, however, in personal values and necessary aspects of value.

Personal values are areas that you as an individual hold as valuable and invest time and money in, but others may not share that same value.

Necessary aspects of value, however, are aspects that hold value and affect everyone's lives regardless of whether they value it or not. Two necessary aspects of value are what we have been focusing on throughout this devotional regarding holistic health. The reality is that someone may not value their spiritual health and connection to God, but that does not mean that it doesn't have intrinsic value or consequences for neglecting that necessary aspect of value or health. If we truly are spiritual beings in a physical body, then we need to take care of these foundational aspects by creating healthy habits to Thrive.

NOTE: The other three necessary aspects of value are:
- Mental / Emotional Health (strength in your thought life),
- Relational Health (the relationships that are closest to you)
- Vocational Health (God's calling on your life).

We will continue to focus on creating healthy habits in the Spiritual and Physical Health aspects, but down the road, you can feel free to come back and work through this process in regards to the other areas of health above.

Challenge to Apply

Take some time to evaluate and write down what you spend your time and money on, (ie, art, entertainment, food, adventure, etc).

Now evaluate the percentage of how much time and money you spend on the different areas of health - AKA the Necessary Aspects of Value.

Spiritual Health (Connection and growth with God) _____

Physical Health (Activity and nutrition) _____

Mental Health (Strength in your thought life) _____

Relational Health (the Relationships that are closest to you) ____

Vocational Health (God's call on your life) _____

Look back at your evaluation of health from yesterday and compare it to how you spend your time and money - specifically when it comes to your Spiritual and Physical health. Does your evaluation of health reflect the time and money spent in each area? Take today and tomorrow to identify ways that you could invest more time or money in order to prioritize your foundational values for holistic health, because the reality is - what we invest in, is what grows.

Extra Reflection

Maybe you looked at how you spend your time and money and realize that you're not investing in the right things. If you feel that way, take a bit more time to reflect before we move on.

To begin, remember that you're created in the image of God, and the things that you love, He put there and also loves! So do not feel guilty about valuing adventure in hiking, or decor, or baking, or a good book - these are not bad! I want to stress that because I spent a lot of years feeling guilty that I loved to travel or go on adventures until I realized God put those things in me! However, what I want us to evaluate today is whether or not those personal values are getting more investment to the detriment of your holistic health. No one sets out to sabotage their holistic health or aspects that have intrinsic value, but it happens slowly over time, until the fallout is painful.

Take some time to see if there is a disconnect between personal values (how you spend your time and money) and the necessary aspects of value. Step back and identify if there are any personal values that are getting significant investment causing lack of health in any of your necessary aspects of value. If so, what actions might need to happen in order to prioritize necessary aspects of value or your holistic health so that you may live life to the full and Thrive?

Dreaming
DAYS 30-31

Verse Challenge

Take some time to read and meditate on Psalm 138. Then write out how God has moved in your life. End your writing time with verse 8, and declare it over your life.

No one can ever really prepare you for when you get a promotion or enter into a new stage of life, no matter how many people or podcasts you listen to. Every change requires readjusting and figuring out that new role. I felt this with each role I took on in vocational ministry, I felt it when I got married and I felt it when I had my first kid. I knew being a mom would be hard work, but the part that I didn't prepare enough for was the sense of feeling forgotten.

It was a huge adjustment for me, leaving a leadership role in the church that had me interacting with a lot of people on a weekly basis to being a stay at home mom. Initially, the newborn stage was a welcomed change, but then the monotony set in. I had heard other moms talk about how they had more to offer than just changing diapers, and now I was in their shoes. Of course you know in your head that raising your little ones is the most important job there is, but in the daily grind you can feel lost - and that's where I was.

I had two babies within eleven months, so that newborn stage dragged on, until I decided to embrace the season that felt barren and make it a season of planting.

One of the hardest things I did when my youngest was 2.5 months old was set an alarm. I didn't want to wake up before them, but I knew I needed to. I knew I needed to get quiet time in the Word to ground myself for the day. I knew I needed to move my body to feel myself again. I knew I needed structure. So despite dreading my alarm, I set it and decided to grow in the monotonous season. That's when something amazing happened. Life started to come back! Excitement and hope

started to rise up again. My passion for life started to sparkle again. But it didn't come easy. It came with a decision to Arise above the circumstances, be disciplined and do what I needed to do in order to Thrive the way I was created to.

Does this ignite a little bit of hope and excitement for your future? I hope so, because that future starts Now!

Challenge to Apply

We're going to take some time today to dream again. Invite the Lord to come and guide you in the next part of this process. Ask Him to be present, give you insight and wisdom as you dream about how the future could look. Ask for His Spirit to guide you into God-honouring dreams that allow you to Thrive as He's created you to.

Consider your Spiritual and Physical Health and write out some dreams that you have for each area of health. Write out in point form or a paragraph how it would feel to be spiritually or physically healthy. How would you view yourself, what would your experiences be as a spiritually or physically healthy person waking up, eating, getting ready to go out, going to work, being a mom, etc. How would being healthy affect your relationships; what would change, what doors would open, what confidence might you experience? And ultimately, how would being healthy glorify God as you went throughout your days and weeks?

Keep The Dream Going

Now just take a moment to reflect on how you feel even writing out those dreams. Take this hope and excitement that's building and let them propel you forward into action in the weeks to come! The things you wrote above really do become your 'Why' which will keep you going when you don't feel like it. So keep these dreams close to your heart.

Created for Order
WEEK 7

DAY 32
Facing Challenges

Verse Challenge
Read Hebrews 12:1-4 and note Jesus' perspective on the cross. What did He focus on when going to the cross?

I've always loved adventure and hiking, but I didn't realize how much I'd love hiking until I moved to Alberta. I remember when I used to think that hiking was a nature walk in the mountains or by some waterfalls. But then I went hiking with one of my friends who was 6'4" for the first time to experience what he considered 'hiking.' His perspective was scaling the side of a mountain until you stood on the peak! I literally thought my lung would be discharged from my body through my wheezing on the way up that steep ascent, but all that faded when I stood on the top of that peak. The view was breath-taking (not just from the physical affects either!)

People will do absurd things just to experience a rush or the feeling of accomplishment on the other side of the grind. And if you're a mom, you know to an extreme degree the intense pain experienced in childbirth, but it all melts away when you hold that little life in your arms.

I love this passage because it still presents the very real pain that Jesus endured on the cross, but also presents His reason for enduring the pain - it was You. In fact, the author said that it was for 'the joy set before him.' Jesus considered the cross a joy; not at all because He enjoyed the excruciating agony of crucifixion, but because He knew what His sacrifice would produce. He is our example for how to face challenges in life.

We will face troubles and challenges spiritually and physically in this life, the question is, what will we do in the face of those challenges? Will we cower with fear, decide it's not worth it and give up, or Arise to the challenge so that we may experience the joy on the other side of the challenge?

One of the ways to help you face your challenges in this journey to Thrive is by re-envisioning what those challenges are. Instead of calling them challenges even, rephrase them as 'opportunities'. It may sound cheesy, but it's amazing the power your mind has over your willingness to act when you rephrase a challenge as an opportunity. I've even heard people refer to their alarm clocks as 'opportunity clocks' to rephrase the start of their day as a new beginning full or opportunity rather than something that startles you into existence.

Another tip on how to face challenges head on is by deciding on a reward or a treat for after certain actions. For example, if you're going to get up early and workout, look forward to your cup of coffee after you've finished. Or maybe you set a goal for reading the book of Proverbs in a month, when you do, you get to go to Chapters to pick out a nice new journal. The rewards don't have to be big, but it is important to celebrate small victories along the way until you reach your destination.

Challenge to Apply

What challenges have you already faced since starting your journey to Thrive? Is there doubt from a spouse, or jealousy of a friend, or maybe kids are pushing back on a new schedule, or maybe the challenge is from your inner dialogue. What challenges are you facing now or what challenges can you anticipate as you continue your journey? How can you rephrase those challenges and face them head on so that you may Arise and Thrive?

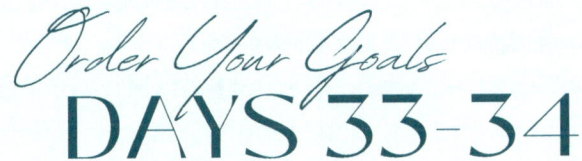

Order Your Goals

DAYS 33-34

Verse Challenge

Read Proverbs 16:1-9. What sticks out to you about your action and God's actions in life?

The past six weeks we have been laying groundwork for our journey forward into Thriving. Setting goals can sound worldly or humanistic, however, when I read about people like Nehemiah, it seems like plans, goals, structure and order can be used for godly purposes. As we've already established, it depends on the motives and the means by which we pursue goals. Hopefully, you've established in your heart the desire to Arise and Thrive for the purpose of glorifying God, and doing so in His strength.

Today and tomorrow, we are going to take our dream that we envisioned last week and start breaking it down into tangible goals, because until we start to plan for our goals, they just stay dreams.

If you're like most people, goals can feel lofty and unattainable, so we don't set them. Or we don't know where to start, so we don't start. However, the fact that you're on this journey indicates that you don't want to just stay where you're at. Rather, you want to Arise from past fear or failure in order to see growth and ultimately Thrive.

There have been many different acronyms used to describe what a goal is from: BHAG's (Big Hairy Audacious Goals), to WIG's (Wildly Important Goals), to SMART Goals (Specific, Measurable, Attainable, Relevant, Timely). The bottom line is that goals SHOULD make you a little nervous and overwhelm you a bit. They should make you nervous because they should be bigger than you. They require you to grow and become a different person than you are now to accomplish them. They make you uneasy because you need to partner with God to grow into living life to the full and the purpose He's created us for. So let me encourage you to Arise, Dream Big and Thrive!

Challenge to Apply

Take both your Spiritual Health and Physical Health dreams that you wrote out last week, and put them into SMART goals.

Spiritual Health Goals:

Specific (What exactly do you want to accomplish, or what would 'done' look like?)

Measurable (What indicators show growth?)

Attainable (Is the goal realistic for this time of life, or what do you need to see it come to fruition?)

Relevant (How is this goal ultimately tied to your Dreams?)

Timely (What is the timeframe you want to accomplish this by?)

<u>Physical Health Goals:</u>

Specific (What exactly do you want to accomplish, or what would 'done' look like?)

Measurable (What indicators show growth?)

Attainable (Is the goal realistic for this time of life, or what do you need to see it come to fruition?)

Relevant (How is this goal ultimately tied to your Dreams?)

Timely (What is the timeframe you want to accomplish this by?)

DAYS 35-36

Verse Challenge

Read Proverbs 3:5-8. Take some time and ask the Lord to speak into your holistic health. Ask for His wisdom and perspective in this journey and commit it to Him.

If you've ever done some running or a race of any kind, you know that it takes discipline in order to cross the finish line. When I trained for a half-marathon, I had a schedule of the different kinds and lengths of runs that I had to do each day. I had a time goal that I wanted to hit, but it didn't just happen on race day, it happened because six weeks before that race, I followed the daily plan in order to achieve that goal.

To start today, take a deep breath and congratulate yourself on setting goals yesterday! Goals can be scary things, as the fear of failure can creep up and cripple us. The beautiful thing about writing down goals though, is that you are a lot more likely to achieve them than if you hadn't written them down. So take a moment to recognize the brave step you took in setting goals!

But having a goal isn't enough to achieve them. Now comes the step of breaking those goals down even more into bite-sized pieces. Now comes when you look at your days and weeks to make a plan for daily action items that will take you to your goals.

Challenge to Apply

To start our action plan, we need to break down how you spend your time. In the space below, map out what a typical day looks like in time blocks. As you do this, take note as to what your days are filled with, because how you spend your time is a good indication of what you're planting in this season and what fruit you'll reap in the future.

	Monday	Tuesday	Wednesday	Thursday	Friday
5-7am					
7-9am					
9-11am					
12-2pm					
2-4pm					
4-6pm					
6-8pm					
8-10pm					

Now that you've written out how you spend your time, look back at it and evaluate if there are time blocks that aren't spent in ways that will produce the fruit you desire. Highlight which time blocks could be used in other ways.

Take some time to look at your days / week and figure out what daily action you could take each day or every other day that would lead to your ultimate goal. For instance, maybe it's blocking out 30 minutes at the same time every day for Bible Reading and Prayer. Maybe it's blocking out an hour four times a week for a workout and shower. Maybe it's scheduling to make home-cooked meals for each supper block throughout the week. Maybe it's scheduling a time on the weekend to meal plan. Maybe it's scheduling 10 minutes each day to read a book or listen to a podcast on a topic you want to grow in. You get the point. The main thing to see change is to make realistic plans that you can do consistently over the course of a week, then a month and then multiple months which will eventually lead towards your goal and Thriving.

One of the final steps in preparation for change is to pick a start date. Take a moment to look at your calendar. As you look at potential start dates, consider what preparation is required to start. Do you need a Bible, a journal, or maybe a new study? Do you need to get a gym membership, or some equipment ready to start? Write out what you need to start your journey below. Once you know what you need to start, then write your start date below.

Items Required to Start	My Start Date to Arise and Thrive!

Lastly, choose someone you trust to tell your decision to Arise and Thrive. Who can you share your action items and start date with? This helps solidify your commitment to making changes to Thrive. When will you tell them so that they may cheer you on and, if you ask it of them, to hold you accountable?

Person: _____

Date: _____

Created for Action
ONGOING

Time to Start!

CONGRATULATIONS! You're here! you've made it to the end, but really, it's just the beginning. The beginning to your journey to Arise and Thrive. You've packed for your journey - the preparation, the planning and the prayer have all led to this moment where you get to take off. If I were with you, I'd love to give you the Dr. Seuss 'Oh the Places You'll Go!' that seems very timely. There will be days that are hard, when you're in a slump, or when you don't win because you're playing against yourself, or when you're in the waiting place. But I want you to remember WHO our God is in those seasons, and WHO He's created you to be. With that knowledge, may you Arise to keep going 'though the weather gets foul,' and may you succeed as you step out in the Lord's power and really Thrive.

As you move forward to the start date you established last week, here are some evaluation tools to help you stay focused on your journey into Thriving as you execute your action plan.

Evaluation Tools

Taking daily steps towards a goal is necessary, but there still needs to be monitoring of progress to see if the action steps are producing what you desire. It's helpful to refocus on your priorities every day, every week and every month so that growth stays at the forefront of your mind. In the pages ahead there are suggestions for daily, weekly and monthly evaluations. Get into the habit to take five minutes every day to reflect on the previous day and the growth you made, the wins you had, the failures or temptations you experienced and how you can Arise to overcome those in the future. Establish now what time of day you want to take five minutes to reflect on the previous day.

Time of Day for Reflection: _____

Now look at your calendar and schedule 20 min in each week for reflection. Put a reminder in your phone for that.

Then schedule a time in a month that you will go through the monthly evaluation.

Daily Evaluation

What is your <u>Why?</u> (go back to your Dream - why is it important to pursue and prioritize Thriving for you personally in this season?):

What were some wins yesterday? Were you disciplined in a certain aspect? Did you stick to your decisions despite emotions of maybe not wanting to do something? How did you grow in your mental fortitude?

Did you have a setback yesterday where you gave into your emotions or temptations? Is there a way that you can rephrase challenges that you're facing to become opportunities? Are you having thoughts of being a failure at all? If so, what truth does God want to speak over you right now?

Take a moment to commit your day to the Lord and ask Him for His presence and empowerment to live honouring to Him.

Weekly Evaluation

What wins did you experience this past week? What are you proud of? Do you see any growth or fruit in your life from your daily actions this past week?

Did you have any setbacks or situations come up that you couldn't control? Is there a way that you can take actions to mitigate those setbacks for this coming week? Do you need to change any time blocks for action items to avoid set backs or conflicts? What changes could you make for this week that will lead to the goals you have?

Take a couple minutes to ask the Lord what He desires for you this week or if He has something for you to do this week. What is it? When will you do it?

Monthly Evaluation

Look back over the month to identify the changes and growth you've seen in a month. How do you feel? How can you celebrate the growth? Who can celebrate with you?

What action items do you need to continue to do in order to see growth or are there actions that you need to change or replace in order to continue on your journey to Thrive?

Are there any thoughts or actions that are negative that you need to replace with Truth? What are those thoughts or actions and what are the phrases or productive actions that you can replace the negative ones with?

Look at your goals, do you need to tweak them a bit to reflect who you are becoming? Do you need to make them a bit more audacious? Ask the Lord to lead you in this process of evaluation.

Manufactured by Amazon.ca
Bolton, ON

31931683R00068